# America's Leaders

# The *White House* CHIEF OF STAFF

by Howard Gutner

BLACKBIRCH®
PRESS

THOMSON
GALE

San Diego • Detroit • New York • San Francisco • Cleveland • New Haven, Conn. • Waterville, Maine • London • Munich

*For more information, contact*
The Gale Group, Inc.
27500 Drake Rd.
Farmington Hills, MI 48331-3535
Or you can visit our Internet site at http://www.gale.com

Photo credits: cover, back cover © Creatas; White House cover inset © PhotoDisc; Sherman Adams cover inset, Alexander Haig cover inset, Andrew Card cover inset, pages 4, 6, 8, 9, 10, 11, 12, 13, 15, 16, 17, 18, 19, 20, 21, 22, 23, 24, 25, 28, 29, 30, 31 © CORBIS; page 5 © Corel Corporation; pages 7, 28 © AP WideWorld; pages 14, 15 © Library of Congress

**LIBRARY OF CONGRESS CATALOGING-IN-PUBLICATION DATA**

Gutner, Howard.
  The White House chief of staff / by Howard Gutner.
    v. cm. — (America's leaders series)
Includes index.
Contents: The executive branch — The White House chief of staff — The chief of staff's responsibilities — Who works with the chief of staff? — Where does the chief of staff work? — A time of crisis — Another time of crisis — The chief of staff's day — Fascinating facts.
  ISBN 1-56711-280-3 (hardback)
  1. United States. White House Office—Officials and employees—Juvenile literature. [1. United States. White House Office—Officials and employees.] I. Title. II. Series.

JK552 .G88 2003
352.23'7'0973—dc21                      2002013784

Printed in United States
10 9 8 7 6 5 4 3 2 1

# Table of Contents

The White House Chief of Staff. . . . . . . . . . . . . . . . . . . 4

Who Can Become Chief of Staff? . . . . . . . . . . . . . . . 8

The Chief of Staff's Responsibilities. . . . . . . . . . . . . . 9

Who Works with the Chief of Staff? . . . . . . . . . . . 12

Where Does the Chief of Staff Work? . . . . . . . . . . 14

A Time of Crisis. . . . . . . . . . . . . . . . . . . . . . . . . . . 20

Another Time of Crisis. . . . . . . . . . . . . . . . . . 24

The Chief of Staff's Day. . . . . . . . . . . . . . . . . . . 26

Fascinating Facts . . . . . . . . . . . . . . . . . . . . . . . 28

Glossary. . . . . . . . . . . . . . . . . . . . . . . . . . . . . . 30

For More Information . . . . . . . . . . . . . . . . . . . . 31

Index. . . . . . . . . . . . . . . . . . . . . . . . . . . . . . . 32

## The White House Chief of Staff

More than 200 years ago, the American government was created by a document called the U.S. Constitution. The authors of the Constitution divided the government into three separate branches with equal powers. The legislative branch was made up of the Senate and the House of Representatives. The judicial branch was the nation's court system, with the Supreme Court as the highest court. The third branch of government was the executive branch, which was led by the president.

Ever since George Washington—the first president—took office, presidents have needed people to help them

*President Lyndon Johnson (front, center) posed with his cabinet in the White House in 1967. Cabinet members are the president's helpers.*

*The president lives and works in the White House. His staff, headed by the chief of staff, also works there.*

run the executive branch. In 1789, the U.S. Congress voted to set up departments in the executive branch to help the president. The leader of each department was called a secretary. Together, the secretaries formed a group known as the president's cabinet.

In addition to the cabinet, presidents have many aides to help them run the White House and govern the country. Some of these assistants help the president write speeches. Others collect information that the president needs in order to make decisions. The president has many demanding duties as the leader of the United States. So he depends on a chief of staff to make sure that the White House office runs smoothly.

*The chief of staff works closely with the president. John Sununu served as Chief of Staff to President George Bush.*

The chief of staff's job was created fairly recently. For more than 150 years after George Washington became president, there were not enough workers in the White House office for a chief of staff to be needed. Most presidents hired a secretary to help them.

After World War II (1939–1945), when the United States became more involved in world affairs, the president's job got more complicated. When Dwight D. Eisenhower became president in 1953, he hired Sherman Adams to be more than a secretary. He wanted him to be in charge of everyone who worked in the White House.

It was Eisenhower who came up with the title "Chief of Staff." A president is not required to hire a chief of staff. Every president since Eisenhower, however, has found it helpful to do so.

*President Dwight D. Eisenhower (center) was the first U.S. president to appoint a chief of staff. He chose Sherman Adams (right) for this position in 1953.*

## Who Can Become Chief of Staff?

Unlike many other government positions, the person the president chooses to be chief of staff does not have to be approved by Congress. The president can hire anyone he wants. Usually, the president hires somebody he has known for a long time and whose opinion he trusts. The chief of staff will work very closely with the president, so it is important that they like and understand each other.

The person the president chooses is almost always someone who has experience in the way the government works. Some chiefs are former politicians who have served in the House of Representatives. Others have worked with the president to run his election campaign.

*President Bill Clinton (left) appointed his friend John Podesta (right) chief of staff in 1998.*

## The Chief of Staff's Responsibilities

The chief of staff is responsible for the operation of the White House. The chief's main duty is to keep track of all the information that goes to and from the president. The chief of staff meets with the president many times each day. He or she must make sure that important issues are brought to the president's attention quickly. The chief of staff also makes sure that other White House staff members have the time, information, and materials they need to do their jobs.

The chief also updates the president on government issues, such as bills that are up for a vote in Congress.

*Chief of Staff Andrew Card informed President George W. Bush of the terrorist attacks on the World Trade Center on September 11, 2001. The chief is responsible for updating the president on important issues.*

The president needs these briefings so he can make decisions about whether he will sign these bills when they come to him. The chief of staff also reviews the president's speeches before they are delivered. He or she does this to make sure that the president's statements make sense in relation to other speeches he has made in the past. Today, the president often appears on television, where he is interviewed by reporters. For these appearances, he needs someone—the chief of staff—to help him communicate with the press.

The chief of staff also keeps the president's schedule in order. He or she helps decide who the president should see or call. This is one of the most significant parts of the chief's job. The president is very busy. Many people want to talk with him, and sometimes it is hard for a president to say "no."

*President Ronald Reagan met with Chief of Staff Donald Regan and cabinet members before his 1987 speech on the sale of arms to Iran.*

*Ronald Reagan met daily with his first chief of staff James Baker to discuss the president's schedule.*

It is the chief of staff's duty to see that only people with pressing business get to meet with the president. For this reason, the chief needs to know what people tell the president in meetings, as well as what the president tells them. For example, when Ronald Reagan was president in the 1980s, he always told his chief of staff James Baker when he met with a visitor without a member of the White House staff present.

The chief of staff's duties may extend even beyond his or her work for the president. As the vice president's job has grown in importance over time, he, too, has turned to the chief of staff to help keep track of committee meetings and to set his schedule.

## Who Works with the Chief of Staff?

The chief of staff works closely with all members of the White House. When a new president is elected, the new chief puts together a new White House staff with advice from the president. This staff includes presidential aides who keep the president informed about decisions made by Congress. There are also assistants, such as the director of communications and the press secretary, who send news stories and other announcements from the White House to newspapers, television networks, and magazines. All the members of the White House staff report to the president through the chief of staff.

*Presidential aides keep the president informed about decisions made by Congress. The chief of staff supervises these aides.*

*The president's other assistants, including the press secretary and advisers, also report to the chief of staff. Pictured (left to right) are George W. Bush's chief Andrew Card, senior adviser Karen Hughes, and press secretary Ari Fleischer.*

Just as the president has people to help run the executive branch, the chief of staff has two assistants who report only to him or her. These assistants are called deputies. One of them helps the chief of staff run the White House office. This deputy may make appointments for the president, schedule trips, and review speeches the president will give. Another deputy gathers news about political matters so the chief can make sure the president knows about issues such as national security, energy policies, and economic matters.

## Where Does the Chief of Staff Work?

The White House is the official home of the president. The 132-room mansion stands in the middle of an 18-acre plot of land at 1600 Pennsylvania Avenue in Washington, D.C. All White House staff members, including the chief of staff, have offices in the West Wing of the White House.

The West Wing is the center of activity at the White House. It contains the president's Oval Office, the offices of his executive staff, and the Cabinet Room, where cabinet meetings are held. The West Wing also houses a press briefing room where the president makes statements and takes questions from reporters about major issues.

*The Oval Office in the West Wing of the White House is the president's office. The West Wing also houses the offices of the president's staff.*

*The chief's office is near the Oval Office so he or she can be close to the president. Pictured in his office is Donald Rumsfeld, President Gerald R. Ford's chief of staff.*

The office of the chief of staff is located directly down the hall from the Oval Office. This makes it easy for him or her to be on hand to help the president at any time.

## USA Fact

Offices for the president and his staff, as well as the Cabinet Room, were located in the original part of the White House until 1902. That year, architect Charles F. McKim designed a plain, two-story office wing that was attached to the west side of the White House. In 1909, the West Wing was expanded to create a central oval-shaped room that became the president's office.

*The Oval Office was part of a 1909 expansion of the West Wing of the White House.*

*Chief of Staff Donald Regan (left) accompanied President Ronald Reagan (left center) to many international meetings in the 1980s.*

## Outside Washington

Because the chief of staff works so closely with the president, the chief often needs to be wherever the president is. Most of the time, both remain in Washington —largely in the West Wing. Other times, however, the president must travel to distant lands or take other lengthy trips. All the time in transit must be used to consult with key advisers, speak to the press, hear briefings on important issues, or do other important work. The chief of staff is often needed at all these times.

### Air Force One

To do his job, the president often has to fly around the United States and to other countries. He travels on a special jet called *Air Force One*, which is also used by cabinet members and leaders of Congress. The chief of staff often goes with the president on these trips.

*Air Force One* is a Boeing 757-200 aircraft. It was remodeled to meet the needs of the president. The flying executive office has 4,000 square feet of space. It includes a conference/dining room, a kitchen, private rooms for the president and first lady, and an office area for staff members.

Air Force One *is a specially adapted jumbo jet used by the president and his staff on long trips.*

*In 1990, President George Bush (second from left) met with his advisers at Camp David to discuss world issues.*

## Camp David

Camp David is a vacation house for the president and his family. It is located about 60 miles from Washington, D.C., in a wooded area near Frederick, Maryland. It has a main lodge for the president and his family, as well as 20 two-story cabins for the president's staff and guests. It also has a swimming pool, bowling alley, and a small golf course.

### USA FACT

Camp David was built in 1942 when Franklin D. Roosevelt was president. He called the new vacation house "Shangri-La." When Dwight D. Eisenhower became president in 1953, he thought this name was too fancy. He renamed the house and grounds Camp David, after his grandson. All the presidents who have followed Eisenhower have kept this name.

Many presidents have used Camp David as a place to entertain visiting world leaders. Sometimes the president holds staff meetings there as well, so he and his staff can get away from the pressures of the White House. At these times, the chief of staff goes with the president to Camp David, where he has his own cabin and work area.

*The chief of staff and other presidential advisers live and work in cabins like this while at Camp David.*

## A Time of Crisis

Richard M. Nixon had won the presidential election of 1968, and in 1972, he was again selected as the presidential candidate of the Republican Party. During the summer of 1972, White House staff members were involved in several highly secretive events. These events led the United States into a time of crisis.

*President Richard Nixon (center) and his staff, including chief of staff H.R. Haldeman, were involved in the Watergate scandal in 1972.*

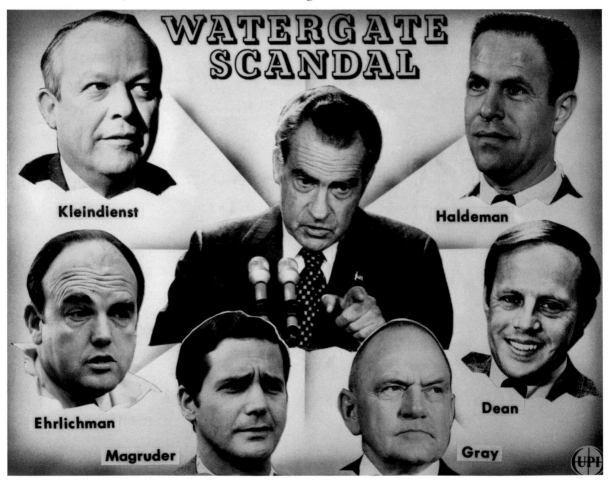

On June 17, five men broke into the Democratic National Headquarters at the Watergate apartment building in Washington, D.C. The burglars were there to fix bugging equipment they had installed during a May break-in. They used this equipment to listen in on private conversations. They also wanted to take pictures of important documents. The burglars were caught and arrested.

*In 1973, Richard Nixon's former chief of staff H.R. Haldeman (pictured) testified at a Congressional hearing on the Watergate break-in.*

That summer, Bob Woodward, a reporter for the *Washington Post* newspaper, got some news from a friend who worked for the government. Woodward learned that White House staff members who worked for Richard Nixon's re-election team had paid the burglars to collect information about the Democrats.

On November 7, Nixon was re-elected. Soon after, the *Washington Post* began to print stories that said some of Nixon's top staff members had helped plan the burglary at the Watergate apartments.

Nixon told his chief of staff, H.R. Haldeman, to tell the press that he knew nothing about the case.

On June 20, 1972, however—three days after the burglary took place—Nixon had discussed the Watergate break-in with Haldeman. This conversation was taped. Nixon told his chief of staff to stop the FBI from investigating the Watergate burglary. He also told Haldeman not to let anyone know that he tried to stop investigations into the burglary.

The *Washington Post* published more articles that claimed Nixon's staff had been involved in the Watergate scandal. In April 1973, Nixon forced Haldeman to resign. He felt that his chief of staff knew too much about the president's role in trying to stop the investigation. Another assistant, John Dean, refused to go and was fired.

Haldeman was upset, but he remained loyal to Nixon. He did not talk about Watergate with reporters who asked him about it.

On June 25, 1973, John Dean spoke to a Senate committee about Watergate.

*Ordered to testify, John Dean, a Nixon adviser, revealed the former president's role in covering up the Watergate break-in.*

He said that Richard Nixon had worked to stop investigations into the burglary. He also said that Nixon had tape recordings of meetings where these issues had been discussed.

The Supreme Court made Nixon give up the tapes. When the tapes were turned over to the Court, though, it was found that some were missing. Others had gaps at critical points.

Under pressure, Nixon supplied copies of what was on the missing tapes. It was

*H.R. Haldeman became the first White House chief of staff to serve time in prison. He served eighteen months for his attempt to cover up his and the president's involvement in the Watergate break-in.*

now clear that Nixon and members of his staff, including H.R. Haldeman, had played a role in the cover-up. On August 9, 1974, Richard Nixon became the first president of the United States to resign from office. Nixon was later granted a pardon, but other members of his staff went to prison. Haldeman became the first White House chief of staff to serve a prison term for his attempt to stop justice from being done. He spent 18 months in prison for his role in Watergate.

## Another Time of Crisis

In late 1995 and early 1996, Democratic president Bill Clinton met with leaders in the House of Representatives to come up with a government budget. At the time, the House was controlled by the Republican Party. The Republicans in Congress wanted to cut spending for certain government projects in education and the environment.

Leon Panetta, Bill Clinton's chief of staff, persuaded the president not to give in on all the cuts the Republicans wanted to make. Panetta had served in Congress as a California representative from 1977 to 1993. He knew many of the representatives who would vote on the budget. He set up meetings between Clinton and the congressional leaders so they could try to reach an agreement.

*President Bill Clinton's chief of staff Leon Panetta (pictured) gave a televised speech in 1996 to persuade the American people to side with the president on the budget crisis.*

*Speaker of the House Newt Gingrich (left) and Senate majority leader Bob Dole led congressional opposition to President Bill Clinton's budget proposal in 1996. White House Chief of Staff Leon Panetta helped them reach a compromise.*

Throughout the fall of 1995, the two sides could not come to an understanding. When the president and the members of the House failed to agree on a budget, there was no money to run the government. The federal government actually shut down for nearly 30 days between November 1995 and January 1996.

The government shutdown made many Americans angry. They blamed both Congress and the president. Leon Panetta went on television to explain to the public why the president could not agree with Congress about the spending cuts they wanted to make. This made many Americans side with Clinton. He and the president also came up with a new budget that they hoped the Republicans in Congress would approve. In January 1996, Clinton and the House finally reached an agreement on the budget that Panetta had so skillfully helped to create.

## The Chief of Staff's Day

The White House chief of staff is a busy person whose days are filled with meetings and press appearances. Here is what a day might be like for the White House chief of staff.

**6:00** AM  Wake, shower, watch television news, and scan several newspapers

**6:30** AM  Eat breakfast

**7:00** AM  Meeting at the White House with the chief's two deputies and the White House press secretary; discuss any issues that have come up overnight, such as national emergencies or economic matters

**8:00** AM  Meeting with the White House staff in the chief of staff's office to discuss the president's schedule

**9:00** AM  Meeting with the president in the Oval Office; the chief of staff informs the president of any sudden changes in his schedule for the day; also informs the president about issues in Congress and other matters that came up at the White House staff meeting

**11:00** AM  Interview with the host of a television news show

| | |
|---|---|
| **1:00** PM | Working lunch with the president and vice president about an upcoming trip to California, where the president will speak on a conservation bill that he wants Congress to pass |
| **2:30** PM | Meeting with members of the president's political party to discuss appearances the president will make at fundraisers in New York and Chicago |
| **4:00** PM | Review speech the president will give at the fundraisers to make sure it matches other speeches the president has made on the same topic |
| **5:00** PM | Meet with the president to discuss the speech and any changes the chief of staff wants to make to it |
| **6:30** PM | Return home; eat dinner and watch evening news |
| **7:30** PM | Handle pressing paperwork |
| **8:30** PM | Phone call from the president; discuss upcoming vote on conservation bill in Congress; agree to set up meetings between the president and several members of the house to see how the representatives feel about the bill |
| **9:30** PM | Phone call to one of the chief of staff's deputies to ask for a report to be delivered in the morning |
| **10:30** PM | Bed |

## Fascinating Facts

**Sherman Adams** served as President Dwight D. Eisenhower's chief of staff between 1953 and 1958. Adams resigned from the Eisenhower administration in 1958 after it was revealed that he had accepted expensive gifts from a textile manufacturer who hoped to get government favors.

*James A. Baker III*

**James A. Baker III** was the only White House chief of staff to serve under two different presidents. He was Ronald Reagan's chief of staff from 1981 to 1985. He held the same position under President George Bush from August 1992 to January 1993.

*President Bill Clinton (left) with Thomas McLarty*

**Thomas McLarty**, who served as White House chief of staff under President Bill Clinton, was a boyhood friend of the president. The two met when they were in kindergarten in their hometown of Hope, Arkansas.

*Donald Regan (second from left), President Ronald Reagan's second chief of staff, resigned in 1987 because he believed he was unable to fulfill his duties.*

After he left his job as chief of staff under President Ronald Reagan in 1987, **Donald Regan** told reporters that First Lady Nancy Reagan had met with an astrologer to help plan the president's daily schedule. He felt he could not do his job properly, and this was one reason he resigned.

**Howard Baker** served three terms as a senator from Tennessee before becoming Ronald Reagan's chief of staff in 1987. When he was in the Senate, Baker was vice chairman of the Senate Watergate Committee. During the committee's hearings, Baker asked a question that became famous: "What did the president know, and when did he know it?"

*Howard Baker*

## Glossary

**administration**—the president of the United States, the cabinet appointed by the president, and the departments headed by cabinet members

**bill**—the draft of a proposed law

**Cabinet Room**—the meeting room in the West Wing of the White House where the president meets with members of his cabinet

**Congress**—the legislative branch of government, composed of the Senate and the House of Representatives

**Constitution**—the document that established the United States government and contains the principles and laws of the nation

**fund-raiser**—a social event, such as a party or dinner, held for the purpose of raising money

*Alexander Haig was chief of staff for Presidents Richard Nixon and Gerald Ford in the 1970s.*

30

*Hamilton Jordan served as President Jimmy Carter's chief of staff from 1977 to1981. He was the youngest chief of staff in American history.*

**impeach**—to accuse a public official of wrong or improper conduct

**legislation**—the making of laws

**nominate**—to name someone as a candidate for a political office

**obstruct**—to make hard to do; stop

**Oval Office**—the room in the West Wing of the White House in which the president works with his staff and meets with visitors

## For More Information

Sandler, Martin. *Presidents.* New York: HarperCollins, 1995.

Baker, James G. *Eyewitness: Presidents.* New York: DK Publishing, 2000.

# Index

Adams, Sherman, 6, 28

*Air Force One*, 16

Baker, James, 11, 28

Cabinet, the, 5, 14
Camp David, 18-19
Clinton, Bill, 24-25, 28

Deputies, 13, 26, 27

Eisenhower, Dwight D., 6-7, 28

Haldeman, H.R., 21-23
House of Representatives, 4, 8, 25

Nixon, Richard M., 20-23

Panetta, Leon, 24-25

Reagan, Ronald, 11, 28, 29

Senate, 4
Speeches, 10
Supreme Court, 4, 23

U.S. Constitution, 4

Washington, George, 4, 6
Watergate, 21-23, 29
West Wing, the, 14, 16
World War II, 6